My Mediterranean Lunch

Boost Your Metabolism And Enjoy Your Meals With Incredibly Tasty Mediterranean Dishes

Dan Peterson

TABLE OF CONTENT

result of the use of information contained within this document, including, but not limited to, — errors, omissions, or inaccuracies.

Pork with Couscous

Preparation time: 10 minutes

Cooking time: 7 hours

Servings: 6

INGREDIENTS:
- 2 and ½ pounds pork loin boneless and trimmed
- ¾ cup chicken stock
- 2 tablespoons olive oil
- ½ tablespoon sweet paprika
- 2 and ¼ teaspoon sage, dried
- ½ tablespoon garlic powder
- ¼ teaspoon rosemary, dried
- ¼ teaspoon marjoram, dried
- 1 teaspoon basil, dried
- 1 teaspoon oregano, dried
- Salt and black pepper to taste
- 2 cups couscous, cooked

DIRECTIONS:
1. In a bowl, mix oil with stock, paprika, garlic powder, sage, rosemary, thyme, marjoram, oregano, salt and pepper to taste and whisk well. Put pork loin in your crock pot.
2. Add stock and spice mix, stir, cover and cook on Low for 7 hours. Slice pork return to pot and toss with cooking juices. Divide between plates and serve with couscous on the side.

NUTRITION: Calories 320 Fat 31g Carbs 21g Protein 23g

Grilled Steak, Mushroom, and Onion Kebabs

Preparation Time: 10 minutes
Cooking Time : 10 minutes

Servings: 2

INGREDIENTS:
- Boneless top sirloin steak, 1 lb.
- White button mushrooms, 8 oz.
- Medium red onion, 1.
- Peeled garlic cloves, 4.
- Rosemary sprigs, 2.
- Extra-virgin olive oil, 2 tbsp.
- Black pepper, ¼ tsp.
- Red wine vinegar, 2 tbsp.
- Sea salt, ¼ tsp.

DIRECTIONS:
1. Soak 12 (10-inch) wooden skewers in water. Spray the cold grill with nonstick cooking spray, and heat the grill to medium -high.
2. Cut a piece of aluminum foil into a 10-inch square. Place the garlic and rosemary sprigs in the center, drizzle with 1 tablespoon of oil, and wrap tightly to form a foil packet.
3. Arrange it on the grill, and seal the grill cover.
4. Cut the steak into 1-inch cubes. Thread the beef onto the wet skewers, alternating with whole mushrooms and onion wedges. Spray the kebabs thoroughly with nonstick

cooking spray, and sprinkle with pepper.

5. Cook the kebabs on the covered grill for 5 minutes.
6. Flip and grill for 5 more minutes while covered.
7. Unwrap foil packets with garlic and rosemary sprigs and put them into a small bowl.
8. Carefully strip the rosemary sprigs of their leaves into the bowl and pour in any accumulated juices and oil from the foil packet.
9. Mix in the remaining 1 tablespoon of oil and the vinegar and salt.
10. Mash the garlic with a fork, and mix all ingredients in the bowl together. Pour over the finished steak kebabs and serve.

NUTRITION: Calories: 410, Protein: 36 g, Carbohydrates: 12 g, Fat: 14 g

Turkey Meatballs

Preparation Time: 10 minutes
Cooking Time : 25 minutes

Servings: 2

INGREDIENTS:
- Diced yellow onion, ¼
- Diced artichoke hearts, 14 oz.
- Ground turkey, 1 lb.
- Dried parsley, 1 tsp.
- Oil, 1 tsp.
- Chopped basil, 4 tbsp.
- Pepper and salt, to taste.

DIRECTIONS:
1. Grease the baking sheet and preheat the oven to 350 0 F.
2. On medium heat, place a nonstick medium saucepan, sauté artichoke hearts, and diced onions for 5 minutes or until onions are soft.
3. Meanwhile, in a big bowl, mix parsley, basil and ground turkey with hands. Season to taste.
4. Once onion mixture has cooled, add into the bowl and mix thoroughly.
5. With an ice cream scooper, scoop ground turkey and form balls.
6. Place on a prepared cooking sheet, pop in the oven and bake until cooked around 15-20 minutes.
7. Remove from pan, serve and enjoy

NUTRITION: Calories: 283, Protein: 12 g, Carbohydrates: 30 g, Fat: 12 g

Chicken Marsala

Preparation Time: 10 minutes
Cooking Time : 45 minutes

Servings: 2

INGREDIENTS:
- 2 tablespoons olive oil
- 4 skinless, boneless chicken breast cutlets
- ¾ tablespoons black pepper, divided
- ½ teaspoon kosher salt, divided
- 8 oz. mushrooms, sliced
- 4 thyme sprigs
- 0.2 quarts unsalted chicken stock
- quarts Marsala wine
- tablespoons olive oil
- tablespoon fresh thyme, chopped

DIRECTIONS:
1. Heat oil in a pan and fry chicken for 4-5 minutes per side. Remove chicken from the pan and set it aside.
2. In same pan add thyme, mushrooms, salt, and pepper; stir fry for 1-2 minutes.
3. Add Marsala wine, chicken broth, and cooked chicken. Let simmer for 10-12 minutes on low heat.
4. Add to a serving dish.
5. Enjoy.

NUTRITION: Calories – 206, Fat –17 g, Carbs – 3 g, Protein – 8 g

Cauliflower Steaks with Eggplant Relish

Preparation Time: 5 minutes
Cooking Time : 25 minutes

Servings: 2

INGREDIENTS:
- 2 small heads cauliflower (about 3 pounds)
- ¼ teaspoon kosher or sea salt
- ¼ teaspoon smoked paprika
- Extra-virgin olive oil, divided

DIRECTIONS:
1. Place a large, rimmed baking sheet in the oven. Preheat the oven to 400°F with the pan inside.
2. Stand one head of cauliflower on a cutting board, stem-end down. With a long chef's knife, slice down through the very center of the head, including the stem.
3. Starting at the cut edge, measure about 1 inch and cut one thick slice from each cauliflower half, including as much of the stem as possible, to make two cauliflower "steaks."
4. Reserve the remaining cauliflower for another use. Repeat with the second cauliflower head.
5. Dry each steak well with a clean towel. Sprinkle the salt and smoked paprika evenly over both sides of each cauliflower steak.

6. In a large skillet over medium-high heat, heat 2 tablespoons of oil. When the oil is very hot, add two cauliflower steaks to the pan and cook for about 3 minutes, until golden and crispy. Flip and cook for 2 more minutes.
7. Transfer the steaks to a plate. Use a pair of tongs to hold a paper towel and wipe out the pan to remove most of the hot oil (which will contain a few burnt bits of cauliflower).
8. Repeat the cooking process with the remaining 2 tablespoons of oil and the remaining two steaks.
9. Using oven mitts, carefully remove the baking sheet from the oven and place the cauliflower on the baking sheet.
10. Roast in the oven for 12 to 15 minutes, until the cauliflower steaks are just fork tender; they will still be somewhat firm. Serve the steaks with the Eggplant Relish Spread, baba ghanoush, or the homemade ketchup.

NUTRITION: Calories – 206, Fat –17 g, Carbs – 3 g, Protein – 8 g

Lemon Caper Chicken

Preparation Time: 10 minutes
Cooking Time : 15 minutes

Servings: 2

INGREDIENTS:
- 2 tablespoon virgin olive oil
- 2 chicken breasts (boneless, skinless, cut in half, pound to ¾ an inch thick)
- ¼ cup capers
- 2 lemons (wedges)
- 1 teaspoon oregano
- 1 teaspoon basil
- ½ teaspoon black pepper

DIRECTIONS:
1. Take a large skillet and place it on your stove and add the olive oil to it. Turn the heat to medium and allow it to warm up.
2. As the oil heats up season your chicken breast with the oregano, basil, and black pepper on each side.
3. Place your chicken breast into the hot skillet and cook on each side for five minutes.
4. Transfer the chicken from the skillet to your dinner plate. Top with capers and serve with a few lemon wedges.

NUTRITION: Calories – 182, Carbs - 3.4 g, Protein - 26.6 g, Fat - 8.2 g

Herb Roasted Chicken

Preparation Time: 20 minutes
Cooking Time : 45 minutes

Servings: 2

INGREDIENTS:
- 1 tablespoon virgin olive oil
- 1 whole chicken
- 2 rosemary springs
- 3 garlic cloves (peeled)
- 1 lemon (cut in half)
- 1 teaspoon sea salt
- 1 teaspoon black pepper

DIRECTIONS:
1. Turn your oven to 450 degrees F.
2. Take your whole chicken and pat it dry using paper towels. Then rub in the olive oil. Remove the leaves from one of the springs of rosemary and scatter them over the chicken. Sprinkle the sea salt and black pepper over top. Place the other whole sprig of rosemary into the cavity of the chicken. Then add in the garlic cloves and lemon halves.
3. Place the chicken into a roasting pan and then place it into the oven. Allow the chicken to bake for 1 hour, then check that the internal temperature should be at least 165 degrees F. If the chicken begins to brown too much, cover it with foil and return it to the oven to finish cooking.
4. When the chicken has cooked to the appropriate temperature remove it from

the oven. Let it rest for at least 20 minutes before carving.
5. Serve with a large side of roasted or steamed vegetables or your favorite salad.

NUTRITION: Calories – 309, Carbs - 1.5 g, Protein - 27.2 g, Fat - 21.3 g

Mediterranean bowl

Preparation Time: 25 minutes
Cooking Time : 30 minutes

Servings: 2

INGREDIENTS:
- 2 chicken breasts (chopped into 4 halves)
- 2 diced onions
- 2 bottles of lemon pepper marinade
- 2 diced green bell pepper
- 4 lemon juices
- 8 cloves of crushed garlic.
- 5 teaspoon of olive oil
- Feta cheese
- 1 grape tomato
- 1 large-sized diced zucchini and 1 small-sized. Otherwise, use two medium-sized diced zucchinis.
- Salt and pepper (according to your desired taste), 4 cups of water.
- Kalamata olives (as much as you fancy)
- 1 cup of garbanzo beans

NUTRITION: 541 Cal, 34g of protein, 1423mg of potassium, 12g of fiber, 15g of sugar, 72mg of cholesterol, 4g of fat, 45g of carbs.

Tasty Lamb Leg

Preparation Time: 10 minutes
Cooking Time : 20 minutes

Servings: 2

INGREDIENTS:
- 2 lbs. leg of lamb, boneless and cut into chunks
- 1 tbsp. olive oil
- 1 tbsp. garlic, sliced
- 1 cup red wine
- 1 cup onion, chopped
- 2 carrots, chopped
- 1 tsp. rosemary, chopped
- 2 tsp. thyme, chopped
- 1 tsp. oregano, chopped
- 1/2 cup beef stock
- 2 tbsp. tomato paste
- Pepper
- Salt

DIRECTIONS:
1. Add oil into the inner pot of instant pot and set the pot on sauté mode.
2. Add meat and sauté until browned.
3. Add remaining ingredients and stir well.
4. Seal pot with lid and cook on high for 15 minutes.
5. Once done, allow to release pressure naturally. Remove lid.
6. Stir well and serve.

NUTRITION: Calories 540, Fat 20.4 g, Carbohydrates 10.3 g, Sugar 4.2 g, Protein 65.2 g, Cholesterol 204 mg

Kale Sprouts & Lamb

Preparation Time: 10 minutes
Cooking Time : 30 minutes

Servings: 2

INGREDIENTS:
- 2 lbs. lamb, cut into chunks
- 1 tbsp. parsley, chopped
- 2 tbsp. olive oil
- 1 cup kale, chopped
- 1 cup Brussels sprouts, halved
- 1 cup beef stock
- Pepper
- Salt

DIRECTIONS:
1. Add all ingredients into the inner pot of instant pot and stir well.
2. Seal pot with lid and cook on high for 30 minutes.
3. Once done, allow to release pressure naturally. Remove lid.
4. Serve and enjoy.

NUTRITION: Calories 504, Fat 23.8 g, Carbohydrates 3.9 g, Sugar 0.5 g, Protein 65.7 g, Cholesterol 204 mg

Grilled Harissa Chicken

Preparation Time: 20 minutes
Cooking Time : 12 minutes

Servings: 2

INGREDIENTS:
- Juice of 1 lemon
- 1/2 sliced red onion
- 1 ½ teaspoon of coriander
- 1 ½ teaspoon of smoked paprika
- 1 teaspoon of cumin
- 2 teaspoons of cayenne
- Olive oil
- 1 ½ teaspoon of Black pepper
- Kosher salt
- 5 ounces of thawed and drained frozen spinach
- 8 boneless chickens.

DIRECTIONS:
1. Get a large bowl. Season your chicken with kosher salt on all sides, then add onions, garlic, lemon juice, and harissa paste to the bowl.
2. Add about 3 tablespoons of olive oil to the mixture. Heat a grill to 459 heat (an indoor or outdoor grill works just fine), then oil the grates.
3. Grill each side of the chicken for about 7 minutes. Its temperature should register 165 degrees on a thermometer and it should be fully cooked by then.

NUTRITION: 142.5 kcal, 4.7g of fat, 1.2g of saturated fat, 102mg of sodium, 1.7g of carbs,

107.4mg of cholesterol, 22.1g of protein.

Italian Chicken Meatballs

Preparation Time: 20 minutes
Cooking Time : 32 minutes

Servings: 2 0

INGREDIENTS:
- 3 tomatoes
- Kosher salt
- ½ cup of freshly chopped parsley
- 1 teaspoon of dry oregano
- Kosher salt
- ½ teaspoon of fresh thyme
- ¼ teaspoon of sweet paprika
- 1 red onion
- 1 lb. of ground chicken
- ½ minced garlic cloves
- Black pepper
- 1 raw egg
- ¼ cup of freshly grated parmesan cheese
- Extra virgin olive oil.

DIRECTIONS:
1. Heat the oven to 375 degrees and get a cooking pan. Coat with extra virgin olive oil and set aside.
2. Get a large bowl and mix your tomatoes with kosher salt and thinly chopped onions.
3. Add half of your fresh thyme and sprinkle a little extra virgin olive oil on it again.
4. Transfer this to your cooking and use a spoon to spread. Add ground chicken to the mixing bowl you recently used, and add egg, parmesan cheese and oregano.

5. Include paprika, garlic, the other half of thyme, chopped parsley and black pepper.
6. Sprinkle a little amount of extra virgin olive oil on it, and mix till the meatball mixture is combined. Form about 1 ½ inch chicken meatballs with the mixture and cut it all to this size.
7. Get another cooking pan and arrange these meatballs in it. Add tomatoes and onions, and blend them with the meatballs. Bake in your preheated oven for about 30 min.
8. Your meatballs should turn golden brown, you can make them more colorful by removing them and coating them with extra virgin olive oil before you continue baking.
9. But that is not necessary. A couple of minutes after this, your meatballs cam is served.
10. No surprises, your tomatoes are fast falling.

NUTRITION: 79 kcal, 74.7mg of sodium, 1.4g of sugar, 301.1g of potassium, 0.92g of fiber, 44.2mg of calcium, 0.94g of iron, 4.1g of carbs, 7.8g of protein.

Classic Chicken Cooking with Tomatoes & Tapenade

Preparation Time: 25 minutes
Cooking Time : 25 minutes

Servings: 2

INGREDIENTS:
- 4-5 oz. chicken breasts, boneless and skinless
- ¼-tsp salt (divided)
- 3-tbsp fresh basil leaves, chopped (divided)
- 1-tbsp olive oil
- 1½-cups cherry tomatoes, halved
- ¼-cup olive tapenade

DIRECTIONS:
1. Arrange the chicken on a sheet of glassine or waxed paper. Sprinkle half of the salt and a third of the basil evenly over the chicken.
2. Press lightly, and flip over the chicken pieces. Sprinkle the remaining salt and another third of the basil. Cover the seasoned chicken with another sheet of waxed paper.
3. By using a meat mallet or rolling pin, pound the chicken to a half-inch thickness.
4. Heat the olive oil in a 12-inch skillet placed over medium-high heat. Add the pounded chicken breasts.

5. Cook for 6 minutes on each side until the chicken turns golden brown with no traces of pink in the middle. Transfer the browned chicken breasts in a platter, and cover to keep them warm.
6. In the same skillet, add the olive tapenade and tomatoes. Cook for 3 minutes until the tomatoes just begin to be tender.
7. To serve, pour over the tomato-tapenade mixture over the cooked chicken breasts, and top with the remaining basil.

NUTRITION: Calories: 190, Fats: 7g, Dietary Fiber: 1g, Carbohydrates: 6g, Protein: 26g

Turkish Turkey Mini Meatloaves

Preparation Time: 15 minutes
Cooking Time : 20 minutes

Servings: 2

INGREDIENTS:
- 1-lb. ground turkey breast
- 1-pc egg
- ¼-cup whole-wheat breadcrumbs, crushed
- ¼-cup feta cheese, plus more for topping
- ¼-cup Kalamata olives, halved
- ¼-cup fresh parsley, chopped
- ¼-cup red onion, minced
- ¼-cup + 2-tbsp hummus (refer to **HOMEMADE HUMMUS** recipe)
- 2-cloves garlic, minced
- ½-tsp dried basil
- ¼- tsp. dried oregano
- Salt & pepper
- ½-pc small cucumber, peeled, seeded, and chopped
- 1-pc large tomato, chopped
- 3-tbsp fresh basil, chopped
- ½-lemon, juice
- 1-tsp extra-virgin olive oil
- Salt & pepper

DIRECTIONS:
1. Preheat your oven to 425 ºF.
2. Line a 5"x9" baking sheet with foil, and spray the surfaces with non-stick grease. Set aside.

3. Except for the ¼-cup hummus, combine and mix all the turkey meatloaf ingredients in a large mixing bowl. Mix well until fully combined.
4. Divide mixture equally into 4 portions. Form the portions into loaves. Spread a tablespoon of the remaining hummus on each meatloaf. Place the loaves on the greased baking sheet.
5. Bake for 20 minutes until the loaves no longer appear pink in the center. (Ensure the meatloaf cooks through by inserting a meat thermometer and the reading reaches 165 °F.)
6. Combine and mix all the topping ingredients in a small mixing bowl. Mix well until fully combined.
7. To serve, spoon the topping over the cooked meatloaves.

NUTRITION: Calories: 130, Fats: 7g, Dietary Fiber: 4g, Carbohydrates: 14g, Protein: 6g

Charred Chicken Souvlaki Skewers

Preparation Time: 20 minutes
Cooking Time : 15 minutes

Servings: 2

INGREDIENTS:
- ½-cup olive oil
- ½-cup fresh squeezed lemon juice
- 1-tbsp red wine vinegar
- 1-tbsp finely minced garlic (or garlic puree from a jar)
- 1-tbsp dried Greek oregano
- 1-tsp dried thyme
- 6-pcs chicken breasts, boneless, skinless, with trimmed off tendons and fats
- Fresh cucumber and cherry tomatoes for garnish

DIRECTIONS:
1. Combine and mix all the marinade ingredients in a small mixing bowl. Mix well until fully combined.
2. Slice each chicken breast crosswise into six 1-inch strips.
3. Place the chicken strips into a large plastic container with a tight-fitting lid.
4. Pour the marinade into the plastic container, and seal with its lid. Gently shake the container and turn it over so that the marinade evenly coats all of the meat. Refrigerate the sealed plastic container to marinate for 8 hours or more.

5. Spray the grill's surfaces with non-stick grease. Preheat your charcoal or gas barbecue grill to medium-high heat.
6. Take the chicken out and let it cool to room temperature. Drain the chicken pieces and thread them onto skewers. (Try to thread six pieces for each skewer and fold over each chicken piece so it will not spin around the skewer.)
7. Grill the chicken souvlaki skewers for 15 minutes, turning once after seeing the appearance of desirable grill marks.
8. To serve, place the souvlaki on a serving plate alongside the cucumber and tomato garnish.

NUTRITION: Calories: 360, Fats: 26g, Dietary Fiber: 0g, Carbohydrates: 3g, Protein: 30g

Mediterranean Lamb Chops

Preparation Time: 10 minutes
Cooking Time : 10 minutes

Servings: 2

INGREDIENTS:
- 4 lamb shoulder chops, 8 ounces each
- 2 tablespoons Dijon mustard
- 2 tablespoons Balsamic vinegar
- 1 tablespoon garlic, chopped
- ½ cup olive oil
- 2 tablespoons shredded fresh basil

DIRECTIONS:
1. Pat your lamb chop dry using a kitchen towel and arrange them on a shallow glass baking dish.
2. Take a bowl and whisk in Dijon mustard, balsamic vinegar, garlic, pepper, and mix well.
3. Whisk in the oil very slowly into the marinade until the mixture is smooth.
4. Stir in basil.
5. Pour the marinade over the lamb chops and stir to coat both sides well.
6. Cover the chops and allow them to marinate for 1-4 hours (chilled).
7. Take the chops out and leave them for 30 minutes to allow the temperature to reach the normal level.
8. Preheat your grill to medium heat and add oil to the grate.

9. Grill the lamb chops for 5-10 minutes per side until both sides are browned.
10. Once the center of the chop reads 145-degree Fahrenheit, the chops are ready, serve and enjoy!

Nutrition: Calories: 521, Fat: 45g, Carbs: 3.5g, Protein: 22g

Mushroom and Beef Risotto

Preparation Time: 5 minutes
Cooking Time : 10 minutes

Servings: 2

INGREDIENTS:
- 2 cups low-sodium beef stock
- 2 cups water
- 2 tablespoon olive oil
- ½ cup scallions, chopped
- 1 cup Arborio rice
- ¼ cup dry white wine
- 1 cup roast beef, thinly stripped
- 1 cup button mushrooms
- ½ cup canned cream of mushroom
- Salt and pepper as needed
- Oregano, chopped
- Parsley, chopped

DIRECTIONS:
1. Take a stock pot and put it over medium heat.
2. Add water with beef stock in it.
3. Bring the mixture to a boil and remove the heat.
4. Take another heavy-bottomed saucepan and put it over medium heat.
5. Add in the scallions and stir fry them for 1 minute.
6. Add in the rice then and cook it for at least 2 minutes, occasionally stirring it to ensure that it is finely coated with oil.

7. In the rice mixture, keep adding your beef stock ½ a cup at a time, making sure to stir it often.
8. Once all the stock has been added, cook the rice for another 2 minutes.
9. During the last 5 minutes of your cooking, make sure to add the beef, cream of mushroom while stirring it nicely.
10. Transfer the whole mix to a serving dish.
11. Garnish with some chopped up parsley and oregano. Serve hot.

NUTRITION: Calories: 378, Fat: 12g, Carbs: 41g, Protein: 23g

Oven Roasted Garlic Chicken Thigh

Preparation time: 10 minutes

Cooking time: 55 minutes

Servings: 2

INGREDIENTS:
- 8 chicken thighs
- Salt and pepper as needed
- 1 tablespoon extra-virgin olive oil
- 6 cloves garlic, peeled and crushed
- 1 jar (10 ounces) roasted red peppers, drained and chopped
- 1 1/2 pounds potatoes, diced
- 2 cups cherry tomatoes, halved
- 1/3 cup capers, sliced
- 1 teaspoon dried Italian seasoning
- 1 tablespoon fresh basil

DIRECTIONS:
1. Season chicken with kosher salt and black pepper.
2. Take a cast-iron skillet over medium-high heat and heat up olive oil.
3. Sear the chicken on both sides.
4. Add remaining ingredients except for basil and stir well.
5. Remove heat and place cast iron skillet in the oven.
6. Bake for 45 minutes at 400 degrees Fahrenheit until the internal temperature reaches 165 degrees Fahrenheit.
7. Serve and enjoy!

NUTRITION: Calories: 500, Fat: 23g, Carbs: 37g, Protein: 35g

Balearic Beef Brisket Bowl

Preparation Time: 0 minutes
Cooking Time : 50 minutes

Servings: 2

INGREDIENTS:
- ½-cup manto negro dry red wine (Spanish or Mallorca dry red wine)
- 1/3-cup olives, pitted and chopped
- 14.5-oz tomatoes with juice (diced)
- 5-cloves garlic, chopped
- ½-tsp dried rosemary
- Salt and pepper
- 2½-lbs. beef brisket
- Olive oil
- 1-tbsp fresh parsley, finely chopped
- 1½-cups sautéed green beans

DIRECTIONS:
1. Pour the dry wine and olives in your slow cooker, and stir in the tomatoes, garlic, and rosemary.
2. Sprinkle salt and pepper to taste over the beef brisket. Place the seasoned meat on top of the wine-tomato mixture. Ladle half of the mixture over the meat. Cover the slow cooker, and cook for 6 hours on high heat until fork-tender.
3. Transfer the cooked brisket to a chopping board. Tent the meat with foil and let stand for 10 minutes.

4. Drizzle with olive oil. Cut the brisket into 6-slices across its grain. Transfer the slices in a serving platter, and spoon some sauce over the meat slices. Sprinkle with parsley.
5. Serve with sautéed green beans and the remaining sauce.

NUTRITION: Calories: 370, Fats: 18g, Dietary Fiber: 1g, Carbohydrates: 6g, Protein: 41g

Grilled Grapes & Chicken Chunks

Preparation Time: 15 minutes
Cooking Time : 30 minutes

Servings: 2

INGREDIENTS:
- 2-cloves garlic, minced
- ¼-cup extra-virgin olive oil
- 1-tbsp rosemary, minced
- 1-tbsp oregano, minced
- 1-tsp lemon zest
- ½-tsp red chili flakes, crushed
- 1-lb. chicken breast, boneless and skinless
- 1¾-cups green grapes, seedless and rinsed
- ½-tsp salt
- 1-tbsp lemon juice
- 2-tbsp extra-virgin olive oil

Directions:
1. Combine and mix all the marinade ingredients in a small mixing bowl. Mix well until fully combined. Set aside.
2. Cut the chicken breast into ¾-inch cubes. Alternately thread the chicken and grapes onto 12 skewers. Place the skewers in a large baking dish to hold them for marinating.
3. Pour the marinade over the skewers, coating them thoroughly. Marinate for 4 to 24 hours.
4. Remove the skewers from the marinade and allow dripping off any excess oil.

Sprinkle over with salt.
5. Grill the chicken and grape skewers for 3 minutes on each side until cooked through.
6. To serve, arrange the skewers on a serving platter and drizzle with lemon juice and olive oil.

Nutrition: Calories: 230, Fats: 20g, Dietary Fiber: 1g, Carbohydrates: 14g, Protein: 1g

Mediterranean Beef Skewers

Preparation Time: 5 minutes
Cooking Time : 8 minutes

Servings: 2

INGREDIENTS:
- Cubed beef sirloin, 2 lbs.
- Minced garlic cloves, 3
- Fresh lemon zest, 1 tbsp.
- Chopped parsley, 1 tbsp.
- Chopped thyme, 2 tsp.
- Minced rosemary, 2 tsp.
- Dried oregano, 2 tsp.
- Olive oil, 4 tbsp.
- Fresh lemon juice, 2 tbsp.
- Sea salt and ground black pepper, to taste

DIRECTIONS:
1. Add all the ingredients, except the beef, in a bowl.
2. Preheat the grill to medium-high heat.
3. Mix in the beef to marinate for 1 hour.
4. Arrange the marinated beef onto skewers then cook on the preheated grill for 8 minutes flipping occasionally.
5. Once cooked, leave aside to rest for 5 minutes then serve.

NUTRITION: Calories: 370, Protein: 60 g, Carbohydrates: 12 g, Fats: 46 g

Cumin Lamb Mix

Preparation time: 15 minutes

Cooking Time: 10 Minutes

Servings: 2

INGREDIENTS:
- 2 lamb chops (3.5 oz each)
- 1 tablespoon olive oil
- 1 teaspoon ground cumin
- ½ teaspoon salt

DIRECTIONS :
1. Rub the lamb chops with ground cumin and salt. Then sprinkle them with olive oil. Let the meat marinate for 10 minutes. After this, preheat the skillet well.
2. Place the lamb chops in the skillet and roast them for 10 minutes. Flip the meat on another side from time to time to avoid burning.

NUTRITION: Calories 384 Fat 33.2g Carbs 0.5g Protein 19.2g

. Beef & Potatoes

Preparation time: 15 minutes

Cooking Time: 20 Minutes

Servings: 6

INGREDIENTS:
- 1 1/2 lb. stew beef, sliced into cubes
- 2 teaspoons mixed dried herbs (thyme, sage)
- 4 potatoes, cubed
- 10 oz. mushrooms
- 1 ½ cups red wine

DIRECTIONS:
1. Set the Instant Pot to sauté. Add 1 tablespoon olive oil and cook the beef until brown on all sides. Add the rest of the ingredients.
2. Season with salt and pepper. Pour in 1 ½ cups water into the pot. Mix well. Cover the pot. Set it too manual. Cook at high pressure for 20 minutes. Release the pressure naturally.

NUTRITION: Calories 360 Fat 9.6g Carbohydrate 29.3g Protein 29.9g

Pork and Chestnuts Mix

Preparation time : 15 minutes

Cooking Time: 0 Minutes

Servings: 6

INGREDIENTS:

- 1 and ½ cups brown rice, already cooked
- 2 cups pork roast, already cooked and shredded
- 3 ounces water chestnuts, drained and sliced
- ½ cup sour cream
- A pinch of salt and white pepper

DIRECTIONS:

1. In a bowl, mix the rice with the roast and the other ingredients, toss and keep in the fridge for 2 hours before serving.

NUTRITION: Calories 294 Fat 17g Carbs 16g Protein 23.5g

Rosemary Pork Chops

Preparation time: 15 minutes

Cooking Time : 25 Minutes

Servings: 4

INGREDIENTS:

- 4 pork loin chops, boneless
- Salt and black pepper to the taste
- 4 garlic cloves, minced
- 1 tablespoon rosemary, chopped
- 1 tablespoon olive oil

DIRECTIONS:

1. In a roasting pan, combine the pork chops with the rest of the ingredients, toss, and bake at 425 degrees F for 10 minutes.
2. Reduce the heat to 350 degrees F and cook the chops for 25 minutes more. Divide the chops between plates and serve with a side salad.

NUTRITION: Calories 161 Fat 5g Carbs 1g Protein 25g

Tender Lamb

Preparation time : 45 minutes

Cooking Time: 40 Minutes

Servings: 6

INGREDIENTS:

- 3 lamb shanks
- Seasoning mixture (1 tablespoon oregano, 1/4 teaspoon ground cumin and 1 tablespoon smoked paprika)
- 3 cloves garlic, minced
- 2 cups red wine
- 4 cups beef stock

DIRECTIONS:

1. Coat the lamb shanks with the seasoning mixture. Sprinkle with salt and pepper. Cover with minced garlic. Marinate in half of the mixture for 30 minutes.
2. Set the Instant Pot to sauté. Pour in 2 tablespoons of olive oil. Brown the lamb on all sides. Remove and set aside. Add the rest of the ingredients.
3. Put the lamb back to the pot. Cover the pot and set it too manual. Cook at high pressure for 30 minutes. Release the pressure naturally. Set the Instant Pot to sauté to simmer and thicken the sauce.

NUTRITION: Calories 566 Fat 29.4g Carbohydrate 12g Protein 48.7g

Worcestershire Pork Chops

Preparation time: 15 minutes

Cooking Time: 15 Minutes

Servings: 3

INGREDIENTS:
- 2 tablespoons Worcestershire sauce
- 8 oz pork loin chops
- 1 tablespoon lemon juice
- 1 teaspoon olive oil

DIRECTIONS:
1. Mix up together Worcestershire sauce, lemon juice, and olive oil. Brush the pork loin chops with the sauce mixture from each side. Preheat the grill to 395F.
2. Place the pork chops in the grill and cook them for 5 minutes. Then flip the pork chops on another side and brush with remaining sauce mixture. Grill the meat for 7-8 minutes more.

NUTRITION: Calories 267 Fat 20.4g Carbs 2.1g Protein 17g

Greek Pork

Preparation time: 15 minutes

Cooking Time: 50 Minutes

Servings : 8

INGREDIENTS:
- 3 lb. pork roast, sliced into cubes
- 1/4 cup chicken broth
- 1/4 cup lemon juice
- 2 teaspoons dried oregano
- 2 teaspoons garlic powder

DIRECTIONS:
1. Put the pork in the Instant Pot. In a bowl, mix all the remaining ingredients. Pour the mixture over the pork. Toss to coat evenly. Secure the pot.
2. Choose manual mode. Cook at high pressure for 50 minutes. Release the pressure naturally.

NUTRITION: Calories 478 Fat 21.6g Carbohydrate 1.2g Protein 65.1g

Pork with Green Beans & Potatoes

Preparation time: 15 minutes

Cooking Time: 22 Minutes

Servings: 6

INGREDIENTS:

- 1 lb. lean pork, sliced into cubes
- 1 onion, chopped
- 2 carrots, sliced thinly
- 2 cups canned crushed tomatoes
- 2 potatoes, cubed

DIRECTIONS:

1. Set the Instant Pot to sauté. Add ½ cup of olive oil. Cook the pork for 5 minutes, stirring frequently. Add the rest of the ingredients. Mix well.
2. Seal the pot. Choose manual setting. Cook at high pressure for 17 minutes. Release the pressure naturally.

NUTRITION: Calories 428 Fat 24.4g Carbohydrate 27.6g Protein 26.7g

Beef and Chili Mix

Preparation time: 15 minutes

Cooking Time : 16 Minutes

Servings: 4

INGREDIENTS:
- 2 green chili peppers
- 8 oz beef flank steak
- 1 teaspoon salt
- 2 tablespoons olive oil
- 1 teaspoon apple cider vinegar

DIRECTIONS:
1. Pour olive oil in the skillet. Place the flank steak in the oil and roast it for 3 minutes from each side. Then sprinkle the meat with salt and apple cider vinegar.
2. Chop the chili peppers and add them in the skillet. Fry the beef for 10 minutes more. Stir it from time to time.

NUTRITION: Calories 166 Fat 10.5g Carbs 0.2g Protein17.2g

Greek Meatballs

Preparation time: 15 minutes

Cooking Time: 10 Minutes

Servings: 8-10

INGREDIENTS:

- 2 lb. ground lamb
- 1 onion, chopped
- 1/4 cup fresh parsley, chopped
- 1/2 cup almond flour
- 1 teaspoon dried oregano

DIRECTIONS:

1. In a large bowl, combine all the ingredients. Mix well and form into small meatballs. Put the balls on the steamer basket inside the Instant Pot.
2. Pour in 1 cup of broth to the bottom of the pot. Secure the pot. Choose manual. Cook at high pressure for 10 minutes. Release the pressure quickly. While waiting, mix the rest of the ingredients.

NUTRITION: Calories 214 Fat 79g Carbohydrate 55g Protein 287g

Mediterranean Lamb Bowl

Preparation time: 15 minutes

Cooking time: 15 minutes

Servings: 2

INGREDIENTS:
- 2 tablespoons extra-virgin olive oil
- ¼ cup diced yellow onion
- 1 pound ground lamb
- 1 teaspoon dried mint
- 1 teaspoon dried parsley
- ½ teaspoon red pepper flakes
- ¼ teaspoon garlic powder
- 1 cup cooked rice
- ½ teaspoon za'atar seasoning
- ½ cup halved cherry tomatoes
- 1 cucumber, peeled and diced
- 1 cup store-bought hummus or Garlic-Lemon Hummus
- 1 cup crumbled feta cheese
- 2 pita breads, warmed (optional)

DIRECTIONS:
1. In a large sauté pan or skillet, heat the olive oil over medium heat and cook the onion for about 2 minutes, until fragrant.
2. Add the lamb and mix well, breaking up the meat as you cook. Once the lamb is halfway cooked, add mint, parsley, red pepper flakes, and garlic powder.
3. In a medium bowl, mix together the cooked rice and za'atar, then divide

between individual serving bowls. Add the seasoned lamb, then top the bowls with the tomatoes, cucumber, hummus, feta, and pita (if using).

NUTRITION: Calories: 1,312 Protein: 62g Carbohydrates: 62g Fat: 96g

Lamb Burger

Preparation time: 15 minutes

Cooking time: 15 minutes

Servings: 4

INGREDIENTS:
- 1 pound ground lamb
- ½ small red onion, grated
- 1 tablespoon dried parsley
- 1 teaspoon dried oregano
- 1 teaspoon ground cumin
- 1 teaspoon garlic powder
- ½ teaspoon dried mint
- ¼ teaspoon paprika
- ¼ teaspoon kosher salt
- 1/8 teaspoon freshly ground black pepper
- Extra-virgin olive oil, for panfrying
- 4 pita breads, for serving (optional)
- Tzatziki Sauce, for serving (optional)
- Pickled Onions, for serving (optional)

DIRECTIONS:
1. In a bowl, combine the lamb, onion, parsley, oregano, cumin, garlic powder, mint, paprika, salt, and pepper. Divide the meat into 4 small balls and work into smooth discs.
2. In a large sauté pan or skillet, heat a drizzle of olive oil over medium heat or brush a grill with oil and set it too medium.
3. Cook the patties for 4 to 5 minutes on each side, until cooked through and juices run clear. Enjoy lamb burgers in pitas, topped

with tzatziki sauce and pickled onions (if using).
NUTRITION: Calories: 328 Protein: 19g
Carbohydrates: 2g Fat: 27g

Quick Herbed Lamb and Pasta

Preparation time: 15 minutes

Cooking time: 15 minutes

Servings: 4

INGREDIENTS:
- 3 thick lamb sausages, removed from casing and crumbled
- 1 medium shallot, chopped
- 1½ cups diced baby portobello mushrooms
- 1 teaspoon garlic powder
- 1 tablespoon extra-virgin olive oil
- 1 pound bean-based penne pasta
- 4 medium Roma tomatoes, chopped
- 1 (14.5-ounce) can crushed tomatoes
- 3 tablespoons heavy cream

DIRECTIONS:
1. Heat a large sauté pan or skillet over medium-high heat. Add the sausage to the skillet and cook for about 5 minutes, mixing and breaking the sausage up until the sausage is halfway cooked.
2. Reduce the heat to medium-low and add the shallot. Continue cooking for about 3 minutes, until they're soft.
3. Add the mushrooms, garlic powder, and olive oil and cook for 5 to 7 minutes, until the mushrooms have reduced in size by half and all the water is cooked out.
4. Meanwhile, bring a large pot of water to a boil and cook the pasta according to the

package directions, until al dente. Drain and set aside.
5. To the skillet, add the chopped and canned tomatoes and cook for 7 to 10 minutes, until the liquid thickens slightly.
6. Reduce the heat and add the cream, mixing well. Plate the pasta first and top with the sausage mixture.

NUTRITION: Calories: 706 Protein: 45g Carbohydrates: 79g Fat: 31g

Marinated Lamb Kebabs with Crunchy Yogurt Dressing

Preparation time: 15 minutes

Cooking time: 15 minutes

Servings: 4

INGREDIENTS:
- ½ cup plain, unsweetened, full-fat Greek yogurt
- ¼ cup extra-virgin olive oil
- ¼ cup freshly squeezed lemon juice
- 1 teaspoon grated lemon zest
- 2 garlic cloves, minced
- 2 tablespoons honey
- 2 tablespoons balsamic vinegar
- 1½ teaspoons oregano, fresh, minced
- 1 teaspoon thyme, fresh, minced
- 1 bay leaf
- 1 teaspoon kosher salt
- ½ teaspoon freshly ground black pepper
- ½ teaspoon red pepper flakes
- 2 pounds leg of lamb, trimmed, cleaned and cut into 1-inch pieces
- 1 large red onion, diced large
- 1 recipe Crunchy Yogurt Dip
- Parsley, chopped, for garnish
- Lemon wedges, for garnish

DIRECTIONS:
1. In a bowl or large resealable bag, combine the yogurt, olive oil, lemon juice and zest,

garlic, honey, balsamic vinegar, oregano, thyme, bay leaf, salt, pepper, and red pepper flakes. Mix well.
2. Add the lamb pieces and marinate, refrigerated, for 30 minutes. Preheat the oven to 375°F. Thread the lamb onto the skewers, alternating with chunks of red onion as desired.
3. Put the skewers onto a baking sheet and roast for 10 to 15 minutes, rotating every 5 minutes to ensure that they cook evenly.
4. Plate the skewers and allow them to rest briefly. Top or serve with the yogurt dressing. To finish, garnish with fresh chopped parsley and a lemon wedge.

NUTRITION: Calories: 578 Protein: 56g
Carbohydrates: 20g Fat: 30g

Garlic Pork Tenderloin and Lemony Orzo

Preparation time: 15 minutes

Cooking time: 20 minutes

Servings: 6

INGREDIENTS:
- 1 pound pork tenderloin
- ½ teaspoon Shawarma Spice Rub
- 1 tablespoon salt
- ½ teaspoon coarsely ground black pepper
- ½ teaspoon garlic powder
- 6 tablespoons extra-virgin olive oil
- 3 cups Lemony Orzo

DIRECTIONS:
1. Preheat the oven to 350°F. Rub the pork with shawarma seasoning, salt, pepper, and garlic powder and drizzle with the olive oil.
2. Put the pork on a baking sheet and roast for 20 minutes, or until desired doneness. Remove the pork from the oven and let rest for 10 minutes. Assemble the pork on a plate with the orzo and enjoy.

NUTRITION: Calories: 579 Protein: 33g
Carbohydrates: 37g Fat: 34g

Roasted Pork with Apple-Dijon Sauce

Preparation time: 15 minutes

Cooking time: 40 minutes

Servings: 8

INGREDIENTS:
- 1½ tablespoons extra-virgin olive oil
- 1 (12-ounce) pork tenderloin
- ¼ teaspoon kosher salt
- ¼ teaspoon freshly ground black pepper
- ¼ cup apple jelly
- ¼ cup apple juice
- 2 to 3 tablespoons Dijon mustard
- ½ tablespoon cornstarch
- ½ tablespoon cream

DIRECTIONS:
1. Preheat the oven to 325°F. In a large sauté pan or skillet, heat the olive oil over medium heat.
2. Add the pork to the skillet, using tongs to turn and sear the pork on all sides. Once seared, sprinkle pork with salt and pepper, and set it on a small baking sheet.
3. In the same skillet, with the juices from the pork, mix the apple jelly, juice, and mustard into the pan juices. Heat thoroughly over low heat, stirring consistently for 5 minutes. Spoon over the pork.
4. Put the pork in the oven and roast for 15 to 17 minutes, or 20 minutes per pound.

Every 10 to 15 minutes, baste the pork with the apple-mustard sauce.

5. Once the pork tenderloin is done, remove it from the oven and let it rest for 15 minutes. Then, cut it into 1-inch slices.

6. In a small pot, blend the cornstarch with cream. Heat over low heat. Add the pan juices into the pot, stirring for 2 minutes, until thickened. Serve the sauce over the pork.

NUTRITION: Calories: 146 Protein: 13g Carbohydrates: 8g Fat: 7g

Pressure Cooker Moroccan Pot Roast

Preparation time: 15 minutes

Cooking time: 50 minutes

Servings: 4

INGREDIENTS:
- 8 ounces mushrooms, sliced
- 4 tablespoons extra-virgin olive oil
- 3 small onions, cut into 2-inch pieces
- 2 tablespoons paprika
- 1½ tablespoons garam masala
- 2 teaspoons salt
- ¼ teaspoon ground white pepper
- 2 tablespoons tomato paste
- 1 small eggplant, peeled and diced
- 1¼ cups low-sodium beef broth
- ½ cup halved apricots
- 1/3 cup golden raisins
- 3 pounds beef chuck roast
- 2 tablespoons honey
- 1 tablespoon dried mint
- 2 cups cooked brown rice

DIRECTIONS:
1. Set an electric pressure cooker to Sauté and put the mushrooms and oil in the cooker. Sauté for 5 minutes, then add the onions, paprika, garam masala, salt, and white pepper. Stir in the tomato paste and continue to sauté.
2. Add the eggplant and sauté for 5 more minutes, until softened. Pour in the broth.

Add the apricots and raisins. Sear the meat for 2 minutes on each side. Close and lock the lid and set the pressure cooker too high for 50 minutes.
3. When cooking is complete, quick release the pressure. Carefully remove the lid, then remove the meat from the sauce and break it into pieces. While the meat is removed, stir honey and mint into the sauce.
4. Assemble plates with ½ cup of brown rice, ½ cup of pot roast sauce, and 3 to 5 pieces of pot roast.

NUTRITION: Calories: 829 Protein: 69g Carbohydrates: 70g Fat: 34g

Shawarma Pork Tenderloin with Pitas

Preparation time: 15 minutes

Cooking time: 35 minutes

Servings: 8

INGREDIENTS:
- For the shawarma spice rub:
- 1 teaspoon ground cumin
- 1 teaspoon ground coriander
- 1 teaspoon ground turmeric
- ¾ teaspoon sweet Spanish paprika
- ½ teaspoon ground cloves
- ¼ teaspoon salt
- ¼ teaspoon freshly ground black pepper
- 1/8 teaspoon ground cinnamon
- For the shawarma:
- 1½ pounds pork tenderloin
- 3 tablespoons extra-virgin olive oil
- 1 tablespoon garlic powder
- Salt
- Freshly ground black pepper
- 1½ tablespoons Shawarma Spice Rub
- 4 pita pockets, halved, for serving
- 1 to 2 tomatoes, sliced, for serving
- ¼ cup Pickled Onions, for serving
- ¼ cup Pickled Turnips, for serving
- ¼ cup store-bought hummus or Garlic-Lemon Hummus

DIRECTIONS:
1. To Make the Shawarma Seasoning:

2. In a small bowl, combine the cumin, coriander, turmeric, paprika, cloves, salt, pepper, and cinnamon and set aside.
3. To Make the Shawarma:
4. Preheat the oven to 400°F. Put the pork tenderloin on a plate and cover with olive oil and garlic powder on each side.
5. Season with salt and pepper and rub each side of the tenderloin with a generous amount of shawarma spices.
6. Place the pork tenderloin in the center of a roasting pan and roast for 20 minutes per pound, or until the meat begins to bounce back as you poke it.
7. If it feels like there's still fluid under the skin, continue cooking. Check every 5 to 7 minutes until it reaches the desired tenderness and juices run clear.
8. Remove the pork from the oven and let rest for 10 minutes. Serve the pork tenderloin shawarma with pita pockets, tomatoes, Pickled Onions (if using), Pickled Turnips (if using), and hummus.

NUTRITION: Calories: 316 Protein: 29g Carbohydrates: 17g Fat: 15g

Flank Steak with Artichokes

Preparation time: 15 minutes

Cooking time: 60 minutes

Servings: 4-6

INGREDIENTS:
- 4 tablespoons grapeseed oil, divided
- 2 pounds flank steak
- 1 (14-ounce) can artichoke hearts, drained and roughly chopped
- 1 onion, diced
- 8 garlic cloves, chopped
- 1 (32-ounce) container low-sodium beef broth
- 1 (14.5-ounce) can diced tomatoes, drained
- 1 cup tomato sauce
- 2 tablespoons tomato paste
- 1 teaspoon dried oregano
- 1 teaspoon dried parsley
- 1 teaspoon dried basil
- ½ teaspoon ground cumin
- 3 bay leaves
- 2 to 3 cups cooked couscous (optional)

DIRECTIONS:
1. Preheat the oven to 450°F. In an oven-safe sauté pan or skillet, heat 3 tablespoons of oil on medium heat.
2. Sear the steak for 2 minutes per side on both sides. Transfer the steak to the oven for 30 minutes, or until desired tenderness.

3. Meanwhile, in a large pot, combine the remaining 1 tablespoon of oil, artichoke hearts, onion, and garlic.
4. Pour in the beef broth, tomatoes, tomato sauce, and tomato paste. Stir in oregano, parsley, basil, cumin, and bay leaves.
5. Cook the vegetables, covered, for 30 minutes. Remove bay leaf and serve with flank steak and ½ cup of couscous per plate, if using.

NUTRITION: Calories: 577 Protein: 55g Carbohydrates: 22g Fat: 28g

Easy Honey-Garlic Pork Chops

Preparation time: 15 minutes

Cooking time: 25 minutes

Servings: 4

INGREDIENTS:
- 4 pork chops, boneless or bone-in
- ¼ teaspoon salt
- 1/8 teaspoon freshly ground black pepper
- 3 tablespoons extra-virgin olive oil
- 5 tablespoons low-sodium chicken broth, divided
- 6 garlic cloves, minced
- ¼ cup honey
- 2 tablespoons apple cider vinegar

DIRECTIONS:
1. Season the pork chops with salt and pepper and set aside.
2. In a large sauté pan or skillet, heat the oil over medium-high heat. Add the pork chops and sear for 5 minutes on each side, or until golden brown.
3. Once the searing is complete, move the pork to a dish and reduce the skillet heat from medium-high to medium.
4. Add 3 tablespoons of chicken broth to the pan; this will loosen the bits and flavors from the bottom of the skillet.
5. Once the broth has evaporated, add the garlic to the skillet and cook for 15 to 20 seconds, until fragrant.

6. Add the honey, vinegar, and the remaining 2 tablespoons of broth. Bring the heat back up to medium-high and continue to cook for 3 to 4 minutes.
7. Stir periodically; the sauce is ready once it's thickened slightly. Add the pork chops back into the pan, cover them with the sauce, and cook for 2 minutes. Serve.

NUTRITION: Calories: 302 Protein: 22g Carbohydrates: 19g Fat: 16g

Moussaka

Preparation time: 15 minutes

Cooking time: 40 minutes

Servings: 6-8

INGREDIENTS:
- For the eggplant:
- 2 pounds eggplant, cut into ¼-inch-thick slices
- 1 teaspoon salt
- 2 to 3 tablespoons extra-virgin olive oil
- For the filling:
- 1 tablespoon extra-virgin olive oil
- 2 shallots, diced
- 1 tablespoon dried, minced garlic
- 1 pound ground lamb
- 4 ounces portobello mushrooms, diced
- 1 (14.5-ounce) can crushed tomatoes, drained
- ¼ cup tomato paste
- 1 cup low-sodium beef broth
- 2 bay leaves
- 2 teaspoons dried oregano
- ¾ teaspoon salt
- 2½ cups store-bought béchamel sauce
- 1/3 cup panko bread crumbs

DIRECTIONS:
1. To Make the Eggplant
2. Preheat the oven to 450°F. Line large baking sheets with paper towels and arrange the eggplant slices in a single layer and sprinkle with salt.

3. Place another layer of paper towel on the eggplant slices. Continue until all eggplant slices are covered.
4. Let the eggplant sweat for 30 minutes to remove excess moisture. While this is happening, make the meat sauce.
5. Pat the eggplant dry. Dry the baking sheets and brush with oil and place the eggplant slices onto the baking sheets.
6. Bake for 15 to 20 minutes, or until lightly browned and softened. Remove from the oven and cool slightly before assembling the moussaka.
7. To Make the Filling
8. In a large, oven-safe sauté pan or skillet, heat the olive oil over high heat. Cook the shallots and garlic for 2 minutes, until starting to soften.
9. Add the ground lamb and brown it with the garlic and onions, breaking it up as it cooks. Add the mushrooms and cook for 5 to 7 minutes, or until they have dehydrated slightly.
10. Add the tomatoes and paste, beef broth, bay leaves, oregano, and salt and stir to combine.
11. Once the sauce is simmering, lower to medium-low and cook for 15 minutes, or until it reduces to a thick sauce. Remove the sauce to a separate bowl before assembly.
12. Reduce the oven temperature to 350°F. Place half the eggplant slices in the bottom of the skillet used to make the sauce. Top the slices with all the meat filling.

13. Place the remaining eggplant on top of the meat filling and pour the jarred béchamel sauce over the eggplant. Sprinkle with the bread crumbs.
14. Bake for 30 to 40 minutes or until golden brown. Let stand for 10 minutes before serving.

NUTRITION: Calories: 491 Protein: 23g Carbohydrates: 30g Fat: 33g

Herbed Lamb Leg

Preparation time: 15 minutes

Cooking Time: 50 Minutes

Servings: 4

INGREDIENTS:
- 1 1/2-pound lamb leg, trimmed, meat only
- 1 tablespoon Provance herbs
- 1 teaspoon salt
- 1 tablespoon olive oil

DIRECTIONS:
1. Rub the lamb led with Provance herbs and salt. Then brush it carefully with olive oil and wrap in the foil.
2. Bake the meat for 50 minutes at 360F. Then discard the foil and chill the lamb meat little. Slice it.

NUTRITION: Calories 336 Fat 14.9g Carbs 0g Protein 47.9g

Baked Pork Chops

Preparation time: 15 minutes

Cooking Time: 30 Minutes

Servings: 4

INGREDIENTS:
- 4 pork loin chops, boneless
- A pinch of salt and black pepper
- 1 tablespoon sweet paprika
- 2 tablespoons Dijon mustard
- Cooking spray

DIRECTIONS:
1. In a bowl, mix the pork chops with salt, pepper, paprika and the mustard and rub well.
2. Grease a baking sheet with cooking spray, add the pork chops, cover with tin foil, introduce in the oven and bake at 400 degrees F for 30 minutes.
3. Divide the pork chops between plates and serve with a side salad.

NUTRITION: Calories 167 Fat 5g Carbs 2g Protein 25g

Coconut Pork Steaks

Preparation time: 15 minutes
Cooking Time : 10 Minutes

Servings: 4

INGREDIENTS :
- 4 pork steaks (3.5 oz each steak)
- 1 tablespoon ground turmeric
- 1 teaspoon salt
- 1 tablespoon coconut oil
- 1 teaspoon apple cider vinegar

DIRECTIONS:
1. Rub the pork steaks with ground turmeric, salt, and apple cider vinegar. Melt the coconut oil in the skillet and add pork steaks.
2. Roast the pork steaks for 5 minutes from each side. Serve.

NUTRITION: Calories 366 Fat 28.6g Carbs 2.1g Protein 25.1g

Beef with Artichokes

Preparation time: 15 minutes
Cooking Time: 7 Hours And 4 Minutes

Servings: 4

INGREDIENTS:
- 2 lb. stew beef
- 14 oz. artichoke hearts, drained and sliced in half
- 2 tablespoons onion and garlic, minced
- 32 oz. beef broth
- 15 oz. tomato sauce

DIRECTIONS:
1. Pour 1 tablespoon oil into the Instant Pot. Set it to sauté. Cook the beef for 2 minutes per side. Cover the pot. Set it to slow cook and set it to 7 hours.

NUTRITION: Calories 505 Fat 19g Carbohydrate 24.8g Protein 60.6g

Beef with Mushrooms & Herbs

Preparation time: 15 minutes
Cooking Time : 8 Hours And 5 Minutes

Servings: 6

INGREDIENTS:
- 1/2 cup garlic cloves, sliced
- 1 cup mushrooms
- 2 lb. beef chuck steak, sliced into cubes
- 1 cup tomatoes with tomato sauce
- 4 tablespoons mixed dried herbs (rosemary, sage, and parsley)

DIRECTIONS:
1. Pour 1 tablespoon olive oil into the Instant Pot. Add the onion and mushrooms and cook for 5 minutes. Add the beef and cook until brown on both sides.
2. Pour in the rest of the ingredients. Season with salt and pepper. Seal the pot. Set it to slow cook. Cook for 8 hours.

NUTRITION: Calories 400 Fat 17g Carbohydrate 11.9g Protein 48.8g

Ita Sandwiches

Preparation time: 15 minutes

Cooking Time: 20 Minutes
Servings: 1 Pita Sandwich

INGREDIENTS:
- 1 lb. ground beef
- 1 tsp. salt
- 1/2 tsp. ground black pepper
- 1 tsp. seven spices
- 4 (6- or 7-in.) pitas

DIRECTIONS:
1. Preheat the oven to 400ºF. In a medium bowl, combine beef, salt, black pepper, and seven spices.
2. Lay out pitas on the counter, and divide beef mixture evenly among them, and spread beef to edge of pitas.
3. Place pitas on a baking sheet, and bake for 20 minutes. Serve warm with Greek yogurt.

NUTRITION: Calories 505 Fat 19g Carbohydrate 24.8g Protein 60.6g

Shredded Beef

Preparation time : 15 minutes

Cooking Time: 20 Minutes

Servings : 8

INGREDIENTS:
- 2 lb. beef chuck roast
- 1 cup onion, chopped
- 1 cup mixed frozen vegetables (carrots, bell pepper), chopped
- 14 oz. canned fire roasted tomatoes
- 2 tablespoons red wine vinegar

DIRECTIONS:
1. Season the beef with salt. Add to the Instant Pot. Top with the onion and frozen vegetables. Pour the tomatoes and vinegar. Mix well.
2. Seal the pot. Choose manual setting. Cook at high pressure for 20 minutes. Release the pressure quickly. Let cool for 5 minutes. Shred the beef. Season with salt and pepper or Italian blend seasoning.

NUTRITION: Calories 431 Fat 31.6g Carbohydrate 4.3g Protein 30.2g

Pork Tenderloin & Couscous

Preparation time: 15 minutes
Cooking Time : 2 Hours And 15 Minutes

Servings: 4

INGREDIENTS:
- 4 cloves garlic, minced and divided
- 1 tablespoon garam masala
- 24 oz. pork tenderloin, minced
- 1 cup couscous
- Dressing (mixture of 1/2 cup olive oil, 2 tablespoons red wine vinegar and 1/2 cup fresh parsley, minced)

DIRECTIONS:
1. Mix the chicken broth and half of the garlic. Pour into the Instant Pot. In a bowl, mix the garam masala with a pinch of salt and pepper.
2. Season the pork with this mixture. Put the pork inside the pot. Cover the pot. Set it to slow cook. Cook for 2 hours. Transfer the pork to a plate and cover with foil.
3. Pour the cooking liquid in a bowl, leaving only 1 cup in the pot. Add the couscous. Cover the pot. Set it to manual. Cook at high pressure for 15 minutes.
4. Release the pressure quickly. Fluff the couscous. Serve the pork with the couscous and dressing.

NUTRITION: Calories 763 Fat 37.9g Carbohydrate 52.2g Protein 54.8g

Braised Lamb Shanks with Veggies

Preparation time: 15 minutes
Cooking Time : 28 minutes

Servings: 6

INGREDIENTS:
- 6 lamb shanks
- 1 onion, chopped
- 1 lb. frozen carrots and potatoes, chopped
- Seasoning mixture (2 1/4 teaspoons garlic powder, 1 teaspoon sweet Spanish paprika and 3/4 teaspoon ground nutmeg)
- 28 oz. canned tomatoes with juice

DIRECTIONS:
1. Season the lamb shanks with the seasoning mixture. Pour 2 tablespoons olive oil into the Instant Pot. Set it to sauté.
2. Brown the lamb shanks for 8 minutes. Add the rest of the ingredients. Mix well. Cover the pot. Set it to manual. Cook at high pressure for 20 minutes. Release the pressure naturally.

NUTRITION: Calories 839 Fat 29.9g Carbohydrate 26.6g Protein 97.5g

Rosemary Baked Lamb

Preparation time: 15 minutes
Cooking Time : 40 Minutes

Servings : 5

INGREDIENTS:
- 1.5-pound rack of lamb, trimmed
- 1 teaspoon dried rosemary
- 2 tablespoons olive oil
- 1 teaspoon salt

DIRECTIONS:
1. Whisk together olive oil, salt, and dried rosemary. Brush the rack of lamb with the rosemary mixture and wrap in the foil.
2. Bake the rack of lamb for 40 minutes at 360F Then discard the foil and cut the meat on the servings.

NUTRITION: Calories 278 Fat 17.7g Carbs 0.2g Protein 27.7g

Roasted Pork Shoulder

Preparation time: 30 minutes

Cooking time : 4 hours

Servings: 6

INGREDIENTS:
- 3 tablespoons garlic, minced
- 3 tablespoons olive oil
- 4 pounds pork shoulder
- Salt and black pepper to taste

DIRECTIONS:
1. In a bowl, mix olive oil with salt, pepper and oil and whisk well. Brush pork shoulder with this mix, arrange in a baking dish and place in the oven at 425 degrees for 20 minutes.
2. Reduce heat to 325 degrees F and bake for 4 hours. Take pork shoulder out of the oven, slice and arrange on a platter. Serve with your favorite Mediterranean side salad.

NUTRITION: Calories 224 Fat 31g Carbs 21g Protein 23g

Herb Roasted Pork

Preparation time: 20 minutes

Cooking time: 2 hours

Servings: 10

INGREDIENTS:
- 5 and ½ pounds pork loin roast, trimmed, chine bone removed
- Salt and black pepper to taste
- 3 garlic cloves, minced
- 2 tablespoons rosemary, chopped
- 1 teaspoon fennel, ground
- 1 tablespoon fennel seeds
- 2 teaspoons red pepper, crushed
- ¼ cup olive oil

DIRECTIONS:
1. In a food processor mix garlic with fennel seeds, fennel, rosemary, red pepper, some black pepper and the olive oil and blend until you obtain a paste.
2. Place pork roast in a roasting pan, spread 2 tablespoons garlic paste all over and rub well. Season with salt and pepper, place in the oven at 400 degrees F and bake for 1 hour.
3. Reduce heat to 325 degrees F and bake for another 35 minutes. Carve roast into chops, divide between plates and serve right away.

NUTRITION: Calories 320 Fat 31g Carbs 21g Protein 23g

Slow Cooked Beef Brisket

Preparation time: 10 minutes

Cooking time: 9 hours

Servings: 8

INGREDIENTS:
- 6 pounds beef brisket
- 2 tablespoons cumin, ground
- 3 tablespoons rosemary, chopped
- 2 tablespoons coriander, dried
- 1 tablespoon oregano, dried
- 2 teaspoons cinnamon powder
- 1 cup beef stock
- A pinch of salt and black pepper

DIRECTIONS:
1. In a slow cooker, combine the beef with the cumin, rosemary, coriander, oregano, cinnamon, salt, pepper and stock. Cover and cook on low for 9 hours. Slice and serve.

NUTRITION: Calories 400 Fat 31g Carbs 21g Protein 23g

Mediterranean Beef Dish

Preparation time: 10 minutes

Cooking time: 15 minutes

Servings: 6

INGREDIENTS:
- 1-pound beef, ground
- 2 cups zucchinis, chopped
- ½ cup yellow onion, chopped
- Salt and black pepper to taste
- 15 ounces canned roasted tomatoes and garlic
- 1 cup water
- ¾ cup cheddar cheese, shredded
- 1 and ½ cups white rice

DIRECTIONS:
1. Heat a pan over medium high heat, add beef, onion, salt, pepper and zucchini, stir and cook for 7 minutes.
2. Add water, tomatoes and garlic, stir and bring to a boil. Add rice, more salt and pepper, stir, cover, take off heat and leave aside for 7 minutes. Divide between plates and serve with cheddar cheese on top.

NUTRITION: Calories 320 Fat 31g Carbs 21g Protein 23g

Beef Tartar

Preparation time: 10 minutes

Cooking time: 0 minutes

Servings: 1

INGREDIENTS:
- 1 shallot, chopped
- 4 ounces beef fillet, minced
- 5 small cucumbers, chopped
- 1 egg yolk
- A pinch of salt and black pepper
- 2 teaspoons mustard
- 1 tablespoon parsley, chopped
- 1 parsley spring, roughly chopped for serving

DIRECTIONS:
1. In a bowl, mix meat with shallot, egg yolk, salt, pepper, mustard, cucumbers and parsley. Stir well and arrange on a platter. Garnish with the chopped parsley spring and serve.

NUTRITION: Calories 244 Fat 31g Carbs 21g Protein 23g

Meatballs and Sauce

Preparation time: 5 minutes

Cooking time: 8 minutes

Servings: 4

INGREDIENTS:
- 1 egg, whisked
- 1 teaspoon cumin, ground
- 1 teaspoon allspice, ground
- ¼ cup cilantro, chopped
- A pinch of salt and black pepper
- 2 pounds beef, ground
- 1/3 cup breadcrumbs
- Vegetable oil for frying
- For the sauce:
- 1 cucumber, chopped
- 1 cup Greek yogurt
- 2 tablespoons lemon juice
- 1 tablespoon dill, chopped

DIRECTIONS:
1. In a bowl, mix the beef with the breadcrumbs, egg, cumin, allspice, cilantro, salt and pepper. Stir well and shape into medium sized meatballs. Heat a pan with oil over medium heat.
2. Add the meatballs and cook for 4 minutes each side. In a bowl, mix the yogurt with the cucumber, lemon juice and dill - whisk well. Serve the meatballs with the yogurt sauce.

NUTRITION: Calories 263 Fat 31g Carbs 21g Protein 23g

Rosemary Beef Chuck Roast

Preparation Time: 5 minutes
Cooking Time : 45 minutes

Servings : 5-6

INGREDIENTS:
- 3 pounds chuck beef roast
- 3 garlic cloves
- ¼ cup balsamic vinegar
- 1 sprig fresh rosemary
- 1 sprig fresh thyme
- 1 cup of water
- 1 tablespoon vegetable oil
- Salt and pepper to taste

DIRECTIONS:
1. Chop slices in the beef roast and place the garlic cloves in them. Rub the roast with the herbs, black pepper, and salt.
2. Preheat your instant pot using the sauté setting and pour the oil. When warmed, mix in the beef roast and stir-cook until browned on all sides.
3. Add the remaining ingredients; stir gently.
4. Seal tight and cook on high for 40 minutes using manual setting. Allow the pressure release naturally, about 10 minutes. Uncover and put the beef roast the serving plates, slice and serve.

NUTRITION: 542 Calories 11.2g Fat 8.7g Carbohydrates 55.2g Protein 710mg Sodium

Herb-Roasted Turkey Breast

Preparation Time: 15 minutes
Cooking Time : 1½ hours (plus 20 minutes to rest)

Servings: 2

INGREDIENTS:
- 2 tablespoons extra-virgin olive oil
- 4 garlic cloves, minced
- Zest of 1 lemon
- 1 tablespoon chopped fresh thyme leaves
- 1 tablespoon chopped fresh rosemary leaves
- 2 tablespoons chopped fresh Italian parsley leaves
- 1 teaspoon ground mustard
- 1 teaspoon sea salt
- ¼ teaspoon freshly ground black pepper
- 1 (6-pound) bone-in, skin-on turkey breast
- 1 cup dry white wine

DIRECTIONS:
1. Preheat the oven to 325°F. Combine the olive oil, garlic, lemon zest, thyme, rosemary, parsley, mustard, sea salt, and pepper.
2. Brush the herb mixture evenly over the surface of the turkey breast, and loosen the skin and rub underneath as well. Situate the turkey breast in a roasting pan on a rack, skin-side up.
3. Pour the wine in the pan. Roast for 1 to 1½ hours until the turkey reaches an internal

temperature of 165 degrees F.

4. Pull out from the oven and set separately for 20 minutes, tented with aluminum foil to keep it warm, before carving.

NUTRITION: 392 Calories 1g Fat 2g Carbohydrates 84g Protein 741mg Sodium

Chicken Sausage and Peppers

Preparation Time: 10 minutes
Cooking Time : 20 minutes

Servings: 2

INGREDIENTS:
- 2 tablespoons extra-virgin olive oil
- 6 Italian chicken sausage links
- 1 onion
- 1 red bell pepper
- 1 green bell pepper
- 3 garlic cloves, minced
- ½ cup dry white wine
- ½ teaspoon sea salt
- ¼ teaspoon freshly ground black pepper
- Pinch red pepper flakes

DIRECTIONS:
1. Cook the olive oil on large skillet until it shimmers. Add the sausages and cook for 5 to 7 minutes, turning occasionally, until browned, and they reach an internal temperature of 165°F.
2. With tongs, remove the sausage from the pan and set aside on a platter, tented with aluminum foil to keep warm.
3. Return the skillet to the heat and mix in the onion, red bell pepper, and green bell pepper. Cook and stir occasionally, until the vegetables begin to brown.
4. Put in the garlic and cook for 30 seconds, stirring constantly.

5. Stir in the wine, sea salt, pepper, and red pepper flakes. Pull out and fold in any browned bits from the bottom of the pan.
6. Simmer for about 4 minutes more, stirring, until the liquid reduces by half. Spoon the peppers over the sausages and serve.

NUTRITION: 173 Calories 1g Fat 6g Carbohydrates 22g Protein 582mg Sodium

Chicken Piccata

Preparation Time: 10 minutes
Cooking Time : 15 minutes

Servings: 2

INGREDIENTS:
- ½ cup whole-wheat flour
- ½ teaspoon sea salt
- 1/8 teaspoon freshly ground black pepper
- 1½ pounds chicken breasts, cut into 6 pieces
- 3 tablespoons extra-virgin olive oil
- 1 cup unsalted chicken broth
- ½ cup dry white wine
- Juice of 1 lemon
- Zest of 1 lemon
- ¼ cup capers, drained and rinsed
- ¼ cup chopped fresh parsley leaves

DIRECTIONS:
1. In a shallow dish, whisk the flour, sea salt, and pepper. Scour the chicken in the flour and tap off any excess. Cook the olive oil until it shimmers.
2. Put the chicken and cook for about 4 minutes per side until browned. Pull out the chicken from the pan and set aside, tented with aluminum foil to keep warm.
3. Situate the skillet back to the heat and stir in the broth, wine, lemon juice, lemon zest, and capers. Use the side of a spoon scoop and fold in any browned bits from the pan's bottom.

4. Simmer until the liquid thickens. Take out the skillet from the heat and take the chicken back to the pan. Turn to coat. Stir in the parsley and serve.

NUTRITION: 153 Calories 2g Fat 9g Carbohydrates 8g Protein 692mg Sodium

Chicken with Onions, Potatoes, Figs, and Carrots

Preparation Time: 5 minutes
Cooking Time : 45 minutes

Servings: 2

INGREDIENTS:
- 2 cups fingerling potatoes, halved
- 4 fresh figs, quartered
- 2 carrots, julienned
- 2 tablespoons extra-virgin olive oil
- 1 teaspoon sea salt, divided
- ¼ teaspoon freshly ground black pepper
- 4 chicken leg-thigh quarters
- 2 tablespoons chopped fresh parsley leaves

DIRECTIONS:
1. Preheat the oven to 425°F. In a small bowl, toss the potatoes, figs, and carrots with the olive oil, ½ teaspoon of sea salt, and the pepper. Spread in a 9-by-13-inch baking dish.
2. Season the chicken with the rest of t sea salt. Place it on top of the vegetables. Bake until the vegetables are soft and the chicken reaches an internal temperature of 165°F.
3. Sprinkle with the parsley and serve.

NUTRITION: 429 Calories 4g Fat 27g Carbohydrates 52g Protein 581mg Sodium

Chicken Gyros with Tzatziki

Preparation Time: 15 minutes
Cooking Time : 1 hours and 20 minutes

Servings: 2

INGREDIENTS:
- 1-pound ground chicken breast
- 1 onion, grated with excess water wrung out
- 2 tablespoons dried rosemary
- 1 tablespoon dried marjoram
- 6 garlic cloves, minced
- ½ teaspoon sea salt
- ¼ teaspoon freshly ground black pepper
- Tzatziki Sauce

DIRECTIONS:
1. Preheat the oven to 350°F. Mix the chicken, onion, rosemary, marjoram, garlic, sea salt, and pepper using food processor.
2. Blend until the mixture forms a paste. Alternatively, mix these ingredients in a bowl until well combined (see preparation tip).
3. Press the mixture into a loaf pan. Bake until it reaches 165 degrees internal temperature. Take out from the oven and let rest for 20 minutes before slicing.
4. Slice the gyro and spoon the tzatziki sauce over the top.

NUTRITION: 289 Calories 1g Fat 20g Carbohydrates 50g Protein 622mg Sodium

Greek Chicken Salad

Preparation Time: 15 minutes
Cooking Time : 30 minutes

Servings : 2

INGREDIENTS:
- 1/4 cup balsamic vinegar
- 1 teaspoon freshly squeezed lemon juice
- 1/4 cup extra-virgin olive oil
- 1/4 teaspoon salt
- 1/4 teaspoon freshly ground black pepper
- 2 grilled boneless, skinless chicken breasts, sliced (about 1 cup)
- 1/2 cup thinly sliced red onion
- 10 cherry tomatoes, halved
- 8 pitted Kalamata olives, halved
- 2 cups roughly chopped romaine lettuce
- 1/2 cup feta cheese

DIRECTIONS:
1. In a medium bowl, combine the vinegar and lemon juice and stir well. Slowly whisk in the olive oil and continue whisking vigorously until well blended. Whisk in the salt and pepper.
2. Add the chicken, onion, tomatoes, and olives and stir well. Cover and refrigerate for at least 2 hours or overnight.
3. To serve, divide the romaine between 2 salad plates and top each with half of the chicken vegetable mixture. Top with feta cheese and serve immediately.

NUTRITION: 173 Calories 1g Fat 6g Carbohydrates 22g Protein 582mg Sodium

One Pot Greek Chicken and Lemon Rice

Preparation Time : 15 minutes

Cooking Time: 30 minutes

Servings : 20

INGREDIENTS:
- Chicken and Marinade
- 5 chicken thighs, skin on, bone in (about 1 kg / 2 lb.) (Note 1)
- 1 - 2 lemons, use the zest + 4 tbsp lemon juice (Note 7)
- 1 tbsp dried oregano
- 4 garlic cloves, minced
- 1/2 tsp salt
- Rice
- 1 1/2 tbsp olive oil, separated
- 1 small onion, finely diced
- 1 cup (180g) long grain rice, uncooked (Note 6)
- 1 1/2 cups (375 ml) chicken broth / stock
- 3/4 cup (185 ml) water
- 1 tbsp dried oregano
- 3/4 tsp salt
- Black pepper
- Garnish
- Finely chopped parsley or oregano (optional)
- Fresh lemon zest (highly recommended)

DIRECTIONS:
1. Combine the Chicken and Marinade ingredients in a Ziplock bag and set aside

for at least 20 minutes but preferably overnight.

2. TO COOK
3. Preheat oven to 180°C/350°F.
4. Remove chicken from marinade, but reserve the Marinade.
5. Heat 1/2 tbsp olive oil in a deep, heavy based skillet (Note 2) over medium high heat.
6. Place the chicken in the skillet, skin side down, and cook until golden brown, then turn and cook the other side until golden brown.
7. Remove the chicken and set aside.
8. Pour off fat and wipe the pan with a scrunched-up ball of paper towel (to remove black bits), then return to the stove.
9. Heat 1 tbsp olive oil in the skillet over medium high heat. Add the onion and sauté for a few minutes until translucent.
10. Then add the remaining Rice ingredients and reserved Marinade.
11. Let the liquid come to a simmer and let it simmer for 30 seconds. Place the chicken on top then place a lid on the skillet (Note 3).
12. Bake in the oven for 35 minutes. Then remove the lid and bake for a further 10 minutes, or until all the liquid is absorbed and the rice is tender (so 45 minutes in total).
13. Remove from the oven and allow to rest for 5 to 10 minutes before serving, garnished with parsley or oregano and

fresh lemon zest, if desired.
NUTRITION: 173 Calories 1g Fat 6g Carbohydrates
22g Protein 582mg Sodium

Balsamic Beef Dish

Preparation Time: 15 minutes

Cooking Time: 45 minutes

Servings: 2

INGREDIENTS:
- 3 lbs. or 1360 g chuck roast
- 3 cloves garlic, sliced
- 1 tbsp. oil
- 1 tsp. flavored vinegar
- ½ tsp. pepper
- ½ tsp. rosemary
- 1 tbsp. butter
- ½ tsp. thyme
- 1 c. beef broth

DIRECTIONS:
1. Slice-slit openings in the roast and stuff them with garlic slices.
2. Using a bowl, combine pepper, vinegar, and rosemary. Rub all over the roast.
3. Place your pot on heat. Add in oil and heat on sauté mode.
4. Add in the roast and cook until both sides brown (each side to take 5 minutes). Remove from pot and set aside.
5. Add in thyme, broth, butter, and deglaze your pot.
6. Set back the roast and cook for 40 minutes on High heat while covered.
7. Remove the lid and serve!

NUTRITION: Calories 393, Fat 15 g, Sat. fat 6 g, Fiber 11 g, Carbs 25 g, Sugars 8 g, Protein 37 g, Sodium 438mg

Greek Chicken with Vegetables and Lemon Vinaigrette

Preparation Time: 15 minutes
Cooking Time : 50 minutes

Servings: 2

INGREDIENTS:
- For the lemon vinaigrette
- 1 tsp. lemon zest
- 1 tbsp. lemon juice
- 1 tbsp. olive oil
- 1 tbsp. crumbled feta cheese
- ½ tsp. honey
- For the Greek Chicken and roasted veggies
- 8 oz. or 226.7g boneless chicken breast, skinless and halved
- ¼ c. light mayonnaise
- 2 cloves minced garlic
- ½ c. panko bread crumbs
- 3 tbsps. Parmesan cheese, grated
- ½ tsp. kosher salt
- ½ tsp. black pepper
- 1 tbsp. olive oil
- ½ c. dill sliced

DIRECTIONS:
1. To make the vinaigrette, put a teaspoon of zest, one tablespoon of lemon juice, olive oil, cheese, and honey in a bowl.
2. For the vegetables and chicken, preheat the oven to 470 F/243 C. Use a meat mallet for flattening the chicken to two

pieces.

3. Using a bowl, set in the chicken. Add in two garlic cloves and mayonnaise. Mix cheese, bread crumbs, pepper, and salt together. Dip the chicken in this crumb mix. Spray olive oil over the chicken.

4. Roast in the oven till the chicken is done and vegetables are tender. Sprinkle dill over it and serve.

NUTRITION: Calories 306, Fat 15 g, Sat. fat 3 g, Fiber 2 g, Carbs 12 g, Sugar 4 g, Protein 30 g, Sodium 432 mg

Simple Grilled Salmon with Veggies

Preparation Time: 10 minutes

Cooking Time: 25 minutes

Servings: 2

INGREDIENTS:
- 1 halved zucchini
- 2 trimmed oranges, red or yellow bell peppers, halved and seeded
- 1 red onion, wedged
- 1 tbsp. olive oil
- ½ tsp. salt and ground pepper
- 1¼ lbs. or 0.57kg salmon fillet, 4 slices
- ¼ c. sliced fresh basil
- 1 lemon, wedged

DIRECTIONS:
1. Preheat the grill to medium-high. Brush peppers, zucchini, and onion with oil. Sprinkle a ¼ teaspoon of salt over it. Sprinkle salmon with salt and pepper.
2. Place the veggies and the salmon on the grill. Cook the veggies for six to eight minutes on each side, till the grill marks appear. Cook the salmon till it flakes when you test it with a fork.
3. When cooled down, chop the veggies roughly and mix them in a bowl. You can remove the salmon skin to serve with the veggies.
4. Each serving can be garnished with a tablespoon of basil and a lemon wedge.

NUTRITION: Calories 281, Fat 13 g, Sat. fat 2 g, Fiber 6 g, Carbs 11 g, Sugars 6 g, Protein 30 g, Sodium 369 mg

Caprese Chicken Hasselback Style

Preparation Time: 10 minutes

Cooking Time: 30 minutes

Servings: 2

INGREDIENTS:
- 2 (8 oz. or 226.7g each) skinless chicken breasts, boneless
- ½ tsp. salt
- ½ tsp. ground pepper
- 1 sliced tomato
- 3 oz. or 85g fresh mozzarella, halved and sliced
- ¼ c. prepared pesto
- 8 c. broccoli florets
- 2 tbsps. olive oil

DIRECTIONS:
1. Set your oven to 375 F/190 C and coat a rimmed baking sheet with cooking spray.
2. Make crosswire cuts at half inches in the chicken breasts. Sprinkle ¼ teaspoons of pepper and salt on them. Fill the cuts with mozzarella slices and tomato alternatively. Brush both the chicken breasts with pesto and put it on the baking sheet.
3. Mix broccoli, oil, salt, and pepper in a bowl. Put this mixture on one side of the baking sheet.
4. Bake till the broccoli is tender, and the chicken is not pink in the center. Cut each of the breasts in half and serve.

NUTRITION: Calories 355 Fat 19 g, Sat. fat 6 g, Fiber 3 g, Carbs 4 g, Sugars 3 g, Protein 38 g, Sodium 634

Grilled Calamari with Lemon Juice

Preparation Time: 10 minutes

Cooking Time: 15 minutes

Servings: 2

INGREDIENTS:
- ¼ c. dried cranberries
- ¼ c. extra virgin olive oil
- ¼ c. olive oil
- ¼ c. sliced almonds
- 1/3 c. fresh lemon juice
- ¾ c. blueberries
- 1 ½ lbs. or 700 g. cleaned calamari tube
- 1 granny smith apple, sliced thinly
- 2 tbsps. apple cider vinegar
- 6 c. fresh spinach
- Grated pepper
- Sea salt

DIRECTIONS:
1. In a medium bowl, mix lemon juice, apple cider vinegar, and extra virgin olive oil to make a sauce. Season with pepper and salt to taste and mix well.
2. Turn on the grill to medium fire and let the grates heat up for 1-2 minutes.
3. In a separate bowl, add in olive oil and the calamari tube. Season calamari generously with pepper and salt.
4. Place calamari onto heated grate and grill for 2-3 minutes each side or until opaque.

5. Meanwhile, combine almonds, cranberries, blueberries, spinach, and the thinly sliced apple in a large salad bowl. Toss to mix.
6. Remove cooked calamari from grill and transfer on a chopping board. Cut into ¼-inch thick rings and throw into the salad bowl.
7. Sprinkle with already prepared sauce. Toss well to coat and serve.

NUTRITION: Calories 567, Fat 24 g, Sat. fat 5 g, Fiber 2 g, Carbs 30.6 g, Sugars 1 g, Protein 54.8 g, Sodium 320 mg

Lightning Source UK Ltd.
Milton Keynes UK
UKHW022219120822
407249UK00003B/80

9 781803 424934